reading level 1.6

Paints   3.0

Come To My Party

Come To My Party

by Stephanie Calmenson
pictures by Beth Weiner Lipson

Parents Magazine Press • New York

To Thea Bardin—*S.C.*
For Ken and Benjamin—*B.W.L.*

Come To My Party

"Happy birthday to me!"
sang Raccoon as he ran out the door.
He was going to find his friends
to invite them to his birthday party.
"Remember," his mother called after him,
"you may invite only *two* raccoons
to your party. Not one more."
"Two raccoons, not one more.
That is who my party's for!" sang Raccoon.
He gave two toots on his party horn
and headed into the woods.

"Hello!" called Raccoon
when he found his two friends.
"Today is my birthday.
Will you come to my party?"
"Sure!" said the raccoons.
"Lead the way!"

As they were walking,
Raccoon saw three bears
he knew from school.
He thought it would be fun
to have them at the party, too.

"Mommy didn't say anything
about bears," thought Raccoon.
So he invited the bears to his party.

At the stream,
four beavers were fishing.

"I bet they'd like to come, too,"
thought Raccoon.
So he asked them.
"We'd be delighted," they said.

"Two raccoons, not one more.
That is who my party's for!" sang Raccoon,
as he marched through the woods.
"Who's having the party?"
asked five squirrels.
"I am!" said Raccoon.
"Would you like to come?"
"Great!" said the squirrels.

Raccoon looked back at the growing line.
"I'm sure Mommy won't mind," he thought.
And he went on singing his birthday song.
Soon everyone was singing along with him,
"Two raccoons, not one more.
That is who the party's for!"

Six rabbits marched up to Raccoon.
"Are we invited, too?" they asked.
"Of course!" said Raccoon.

They were hurrying along when
seven groundhogs poked up their heads.
"Where is everyone going?" they asked.
"To my birthday party," said Raccoon.
"Follow us!"

Eight porcupines tried to get untangled
when they heard the news.
"We'll be there in a minute!" they called.

Nine frogs leaped off their lily pads.
"We won't take up much room," they said.

Ten ducks waddled up
from the stream, quacking,
"Two raccoons, not one more.
That is who the party's for!"
And they joined the line.

Finally, Raccoon reached his house.
"Mommy, I'm home!" he called.
Mrs. Raccoon came out to welcome him.
When she saw how many animals there were,
her mouth dropped open and
she turned a funny color green.
"Are you all right, Mommy?" asked Raccoon.

As soon as Mrs. Raccoon could speak,
she whispered,
"Didn't I say *two* raccoons, not one more?"
"Count them, Mommy.
There really are only two," said Raccoon.
Mrs. Raccoon counted.
"One. Two. You are right," she said.
"There are two raccoons."
And she moved the party outside.

Everyone had a wonderful time
— raccoons, bears, beavers,
squirrels, rabbits, groundhogs,
porcupines, frogs, and ducks.
"Happy birthday, Raccoon," they sang.
"Happy birthday to you!"

Do you know how many animals
came to Raccoon's party?

2 raccoons
3 bears
4 beavers
5 squirrels
6 rabbits
7 groundhogs
8 porcupines
9 frogs
10 ducks

_____

54 animals in all!

About the Author

STEPHANIE CALMENSON is the author of many popular books for children, including *Where Am I?: Very First Riddles, The Principal's New Clothes, Dinner at the Panda Palace,* and for Parents, *One Little Monkey, Where Will the Animals Stay?,* and *The Little Witch Sisters.*

Before turning to writing full-time, she was an elementary school teacher, and a children's book editor.

Stephanie Calmenson wishes all her readers a very happy birthday.

About the Artist

BETH WEINER LIPSON, a graduate of the Rhode Island School of Design, has illustrated over twenty books for children. Ms. Lipson knew very early that she wanted to be a children's book illustrator. She submitted her first drawings to a New York publisher when she was only twelve years old.

While Ms. Lipson was working on *Come To My Party,* there was a true "birth-day". Halfway through the book, the illustrator gave birth to her first child, Benjamin.

Ms. Lipson lives in New York City with her husband, Ken, and Benjamin.